ST. PAUL'S JOURNEYS IN THE GREEK ORIENT

STUDIES IN BIBLICAL ARCHAEOLOGY NO. 4

ST. PAUL'S JOURNEYS IN THE GREEK ORIENT

HENRI METZGER

*Former member of the French School in Athens
and of the French Institute at Istanbul,
Lecturer at the University of Lyons*

PHILOSOPHICAL LIBRARY
NEW YORK

4763

Translated by Professor S. H. Hooke
from the French
LES ROUTES DE SAINT PAUL DANS L'ORIENT GREC
(*Delachaux & Niestlé, Neuchâtel 1954*)

Published 1955, by the Philosophical Library, Inc.,
15 East 40th Street, New York, 16, N.Y.

Printed in Great Britain for Philosophical Library, Inc., by
The Camelot Press Ltd., London and Southampton

CONTENTS

LIST OF ILLUSTRATIONS

We are indebted to M. F. Amadry for the photograph of Plate 3, M. J. Lassus for the photograph of Plate 2, M. R. Matton for the photographs of Plates 6, 7 and 10. The other photographs, except Plate 1, were taken by the author.

PREFACE

In the spring of 1946, while I was travelling in western and southern Anatolia, I had occasion to make a journey by sea from Smyrna to Adalia. The steamer *Erzurun*, in which I had booked my passage, sailed up every inlet and put in at every port, so that this sea-trip of four days enabled me to become acquainted for the first time with the mainland of Asia Minor and its Aegean extensions. I was aware that on my left lay Ephesus, Miletus, Didymus, and Cnidus, while on my right lay islands bearing the magical names of Samos, Cos, and Rhodes. In the book of Acts I read once again, as our ship traversed them, the account of the stages of St. Paul's journey, from the shores of the Troad as far as Caesarea Philippi at the end of his third missionary journey, and as I read, the sacred story glowed with new illumination. Leaving the boat at Adalia, I was taken the same day by my colleagues of the University of Stambul to Perga, where I found fresh traces of the apostle. Somewhat later on we climbed up into Pisidia, and came upon Antioch. Still later we traversed the Greek stages of the Pauline itinerary, and, quite recently, visited Patara, Myra, and Iconium. These journeys gave me the idea of writing this little book.

The circumstances which gave birth to the book have prescribed its limits. Even had I been able, I have never intended to write a critical commentary on the text of Acts: what I have attempted to do is to give a very brief commentary on the narrative of St. Paul's three missionary journeys in Asia Minor and in Greece, and of his journey as a prisoner from Jerusalem to Rome. I have not concerned myself either with his stay in Syria or in Palestine, or with any labours which he may have been able to carry out in Rome or in the Roman West. My only aim has been to give a picture of the apostle's missionary horizon, to describe the countries which he traversed and the peoples to whom he preached his gospel, hoping that by this means the modern reader may be enabled to follow his trail through the Greek orient.

I

THE GREEK ORIENT IN THE TIME OF ST. PAUL

Although its political organization was Roman, and much of its population was only slightly hellenized and still retained its local characteristics and cults, the world to which St. Paul's message was addressed presents itself to us at first sight as a Greek world. Provincial administration, civic organization, and even social customs, retained their Greek stamp. Although, in some districts of Asia Minor and Syria, local dialects persisted, it was Greek and not Latin which was the language of common intercourse. Paul, himself a Roman citizen and a native of Tarsus in Cilicia, nevertheless habitually expressed himself in Greek (Pl. 1). To such an extent had the gods of the Hellenic pantheon, in various ways, either replaced or become assimilated to the ancient local deities, that a common religion pervaded all the urban centres of the eastern Mediterranean.

The conquests of Alexander and the government of the Diadochi and the Epigoni[1] had made Roman

[1] This is the designation of the generals who divided between them the heritage of the Macedonian conqueror, and who founded permanent dynasties.

unity possible. While the successors of Antigonus ruled over Macedonia and Greece, the Seleucids retained control of Asia Minor, Syria, and the eastern satrapies of the Persian Empire, and the Lagids retained that of Egypt. This balance of power, unstable though it was, persisted during the greater part of the third century, but soon the vast empire of the Seleucids began to disintegrate, suffering the loss of most of its eastern provinces and even some parts of Anatolia. On the other hand, Roman intervention, set in motion by the Senate intentionally or otherwise, was destined gradually to sap Macedonian rule in Greece, and to drive the Seleucids out of Asia Minor. By the middle of the second century Greece, Macedonia, and western Anatolia had become Roman provinces. In the first century the same fate befell Bithynia, Cilicia, and Syria. When Augustus assumed the reins of power central Asia Minor in its turn became part of the empire with the name of the province of Galatia;[1] in the reign of Claudius, Lycia and Pamphylia suffered a similar fate. Meanwhile the Egypt of the Lagids had also ceased to be an independent state.

Thus, in the period of St. Paul's missionary journeys, the Roman conquest of the Greek Orient was practically complete, and the apostle's preaching could profit by the very considerable advantages

[1] To be distinguished from Galatia in the strict meaning of the term, or from the 'Galatic region'.

which accrued from the Roman peace. First of all
there were the roads. Although not all the credit
for them should be given to the Roman government, since in Asia Minor some of the roads go
back to the period of Persian rule (fourth–sixth centuries B.C.), while others belong to the Seleucid
period, nevertheless, in the Greek or Anatolian
countries, ravaged by centuries of warfare, Roman
road-building activities had brought about striking
improvements. People were encouraged to travel by
the excellent condition of the overland routes and
their almost complete safety: 'In fact, travel was of
frequent occurrence. Delegates and petitioners were
on their way to present themselves before the emperor or the Senate at Rome, or before the governor
or the provincial assemblies in the provincial capitals. There were procurators and officials returning
to their posts; pilgrims visiting the holy places of
Asia Minor and Egypt; sick persons seeking the
help of Aesculapius; doctors, rhetoricians, sophists,
Dionysiac artists, journeying from city to city to sell
their knowledge or their skill; students bound for
Athens, Pergamum, Rhodes, Tarsus, Syrian Antioch,
or Alexandria in quest of learning; athletes seeking
to win crowns at the great games; Cynic and Stoic
teachers, mendicant monks of Cybele, prophets,
diviners and quacks, merchants of every kind,
archaeologists, plain tourists, to say nothing of Jews
who found communities of their fellow-countrymen
almost everywhere they went: such were the crowds

that thronged the imperial roads in every direction.'[1]

Nor was the sea-borne traffic less dense, when once the extinction of piracy had restored the safety of the sea routes. From shore to shore of the Mediterranean, from Egypt to Asia Minor, and from Syria to Italy, at least during the fine weather season, an incessant movement of ships produced a constantly recurring interchange of populations. The ports of Alexandria, Ephesus, Corinth, Thessalonica, or Rhodes were crowded with foreign merchants, who have often been compared with those of the great modern Levantine cities such as Beirut, Alexandria, or Smyrna, and among these traders the Jews of the Diaspora occupied a special place.

The long succession of disasters which had befallen Palestine had for a considerable period been forcing the Jews to seek refuge in other lands. At the beginning of the Christian era we find them scattered in considerable numbers throughout the whole Greco-Roman world. All these Jews persisted in regarding Jerusalem as their religious capital, and in paying the Temple Tax. The Roman government guaranteed their right to collect and transmit this money. Legally these Jews of the Diaspora were 'aliens', and as such enjoyed the protection of the law, which permitted them to make their synagogues centres of religious corporations, possessing their own tribunals. Many of them had acquired citizenship, especially in the Syrian kingdom of the Seleucids. Later on

[1] Festugière, *Le monde gréco-romain au temps de Notre Seigneur*, I, p. 20.

others were granted the privilege of Roman citizenship.

It is incontestable that the spread of these Jewish colonies, together with the administrative unity of the Roman empire, presented most favourable circumstances for the work of St. Paul. Nevertheless, there has been, perhaps, a tendency to exaggerate the importance of the Diaspora. Although the Pauline preaching never ignored them, it never confined itself to the Jewish communities. It addressed itself as much to the populace of the great urban centres as to those of the high Anatolian plateaux and the Macedonian plains, and this threefold distribution has its own significance. Neither the great trading centres such as Antioch, Ephesus, or Corinth, still less the countryside of Asia Minor or Macedonia, possessed a Jewish population in the strict sense of the word; nor on the other hand could they be said to have possessed a predominantly Hellenic population; the prevailing element was indigenous or cosmopolitan. In a world already unified by the successors of Alexander before Rome had accomplished it, St. Paul seems to have felt a certain mistrust of purely Greek localities. Perhaps he had a vague sense that the concept of 'citizen', based on that of the Hellenic *polis*, constituted a most serious obstacle to the propagation of a religion which refused to accept the limits of citizenship. To the Greek citizen, bound by ancestral ties to his city cults, a universal religion was no more attractive than it was to the Jew with his ancient covenant. The Pauline gospel was destined to find a far more favourable soil among foreigners, countryfolk, or those who lived beyond the reign of law.

1. St. Paul as a missionary (Ravenna mosaic)

2 (*a*). The Orontes at Antioch

2 (*b*). Paphos (Cyprus)

II

ST. PAUL'S FIRST MISSIONARY JOURNEY

Antioch. 'Now there were at Antioch, in the church that was there, prophets and teachers . . . and as they ministered to the Lord . . . the Holy Spirit said, Separate me Barnabas and Saul for the work whereunto I have called them. Then, when they had fasted and prayed and laid their hands upon them, they sent them away. So they, being sent forth by the Holy Spirit, went down to Seleucia; and from thence they sailed to Cyprus.'

Thus does the book of Acts (13.1-4) describe the start of the first missionary journey. It may be recalled that St. Paul, after his conversion and his visit to the Church of Jerusalem, had withdrawn to his native city, Tarsus. We know nothing about this period of retirement which certainly could not have been one of inaction, since Barnabas went to fetch him, thirteen years later, to bring him to Antioch (Pl. 2a). Meanwhile the Christian message had reached the ancient capital of the Seleucids which enjoyed throughout the Orient the reputation of a great and wealthy city, famous for its theatre and

its games. It was at Antioch that the disciples received
the name of Christians, and it was here that the con-
ception of the Gentile mission was born; in such an
atmosphere did the future apostle of the Gentiles
spend a formative year.

Cyprus. At the eventful moment when the two
missionaries, accompanied at the outset of their
journey by John Mark, left Antioch and embarked
at Seleucia, the new religion had scarcely penetrated
beyond Syria and possibly Cyprus. Hence their departure marks the real beginning of the Christian
mission and of St. Paul's missionary career. It was
with no sense of having reached alien soil that St.
Paul and his companions landed in Cyprus. The
majestic background, the warm golden light, and
even the vegetation, would remind the travellers of
Syria and Cilicia which they had lately left. Still
more reminiscent were the very ancient Phoenician
settlements which they found on the southern coast
of the island, such as Salamis, Amathonthis, and
above all Paphos (Pl. 2*b*), whence of old the cult of
Aphrodite, goddess of reborn vegetation, had spread
across the Greek world as far as Sicily. Lying at the
meeting-place of the sea routes leading to Syria, Asia
Minor, and Greece, Cyprus seemed the inevitable
first stage of a missionary venture. But it was only
a stage; St. Paul's gaze was directed towards the
future: at Paphos he embarked once more, this time
for Anatolia. At that time this seat of a very ancient
civilization was in no sense a geographical unity;

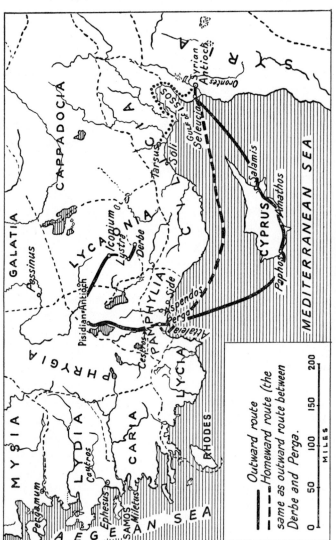

I. ST. PAUL'S FIRST MISSIONARY JOURNEY

each of its constituent provinces retained its own characteristic features.

Asia Minor in the first century of the Christian Era. Asia Minor, the cradle of the Phrygian and Hittite civilizations, had attracted Greek colonists from a very early date. All along the Aegean coast rich trading cities had sprung into being; at a time when Athens and Sparta were still only insignificant provincial capitals, Ephesus, Miletus, Clazomenos, and Phocea were becoming the centres of a brilliant culture whose influence was destined to be felt from Etruria to Egypt and the Tauric Chersonese. In the course of its history Asia Minor had experienced the Persian occupation, a purely military rule which does not seem to have left any abiding vestiges. Alexander's conquests brought it again for several centuries within the sphere of Hellenism, but Greek influence, however, never penetrated beyond the coastal regions. On their first arrival the Romans were content to gain a footing in the western part of the peninsula, which they made into their province of Asia; at the outset of our era they were beginning to advance into the rest of the country, where they occupied the coasts and the ports, and established military colonies in strategic points dominating the interior. At the point of time when Paul landed in Pamphylia this expansion was far from complete, and it was not until the age of the Antonines in the second century that the whole of Anatolia enjoyed the blessings of the Roman peace.

If the spread of Hellenism had been unhindered among the urban populations of the western and southern coasts and had created there, in the period with which we are concerned, centres of civilization more fertile than Athens or Alexandria, as the names of Apollonius of Perga, Dionysius or Halicarnassus, Epictetus, and Strabo attest, it is an indication that Hellenism must have penetrated into the interior and profoundly altered the character of the country. Certainly Greek had prevailed over Lydian in the province of Asia, but the local dialects still persisted in many districts. We know that the emperor Claudius deprived a well-known Lydian of Roman citizenship because he was ignorant of Latin. The difficulties of intercommunication and the severity of the winter climate interposed barriers between the inhabitants of the various provinces which tended to enhance the extreme diversity of cults. It was only the important cities which accepted the great gods of the Greek pantheon, Dionysus, Aesculapius, Aphrodite, Tyché, or sought to excel one another in the sycophancy of the homage which they offered to the emperor, the empress, or the deity of Rome; the countryfolk continued to worship their local gods, paying tribute to the intrusive Hellenism by finding Greek counterparts for them. The triad worshipped by the Pisidian hill-dwellers became the group of Helen between the Dioscuri; a huntress deity accompanied by a boar or a stag became Artemis; a horseman with a club was Hercules; musicians might be equated with the Muses, but no one would be taken in by these disguises.

Moreover, some of these cults were carried by fanatical converts beyond the bounds of their homeland and enjoyed a vast popularity. Such was the fortune of the great Phrygian Mother who, borne from the remote fastnesses of Pessinus, reached the Aegean shores and found frenzied devotees even in Rome. Asia Minor, already a country of ecstatic religions with strange and barbaric rituals, was also to become the home of wonder-workers, philosophers, and charlatans. The dwellers by the Euxine shores were to be bamboozled by the vulgar trickeries of Alexander of Abonoteichos who caused the serpent of Aesculapius to appear before a deluded crowd. A certain Artemidorus of Ephesus or Daldis was to devote an entire book to the interpretation of dreams under the title 'The Key of Dreams'. Aelius Aristides, the sick devotee of Aesculapius, was to pour out a flood of treatises describing in glowing terms the unexpected care lavished upon him by the learned priests of Pergamum.

Pamphylia. Such was the strange and baffling atmosphere into which St. Paul was to be plunged in the course of his extended Anatolian journeys. In Pamphylia, where he landed, he found a country which strongly resembled, in soil, culture, and civilization, the land of his birth. It is an extensive plain, bounded on the north by the Pisidian Taurus, on the west by the Lycian mountains, and on the east by those of Cilicia. It is sheltered from the north winds, generously watered by the Cestrus, the Eurymedon, and the Melas, and well irrigated by the numerous aqueducts built by the Roman government. In the first century of our era, Pamphylia embraced five great cities, two on the coast, Attaleia and Sidé, and three in the interior, Perga, Sillyon and Aspendos. Attaleia alone of these flourishing cities has survived in the modern Adalia, one of the enchanting localities of Anatolia. Nothing is to be found elsewhere but vast heaps of ruins, often buried under vegetation. Here and there at sparse intervals the solitude is broken by the black goat's hair tent of a Yürük shepherd; or a caravan of camels may be seen following the track of some ancient road; but nothing could be more arresting than the contrast between the majestic ruins, unpillaged by any modern search for marble, and the utter silence of the surrounding landscape. Here, three leagues from the coast, lies Perga, the ancient religious capital of Pamphylia, the centre of a cult of Artemis which rivalled that of Ephesus. The temple of the patron-goddess has not been unearthed, but it is still possible to pass along the main street of the city, about thirty metres wide, once bordered by covered galleries like the arcades of Italian cities. The theatre and the stadum lay outside the walls at the foot of an eminence; from their upper tiers it is possible to survey the whole extent of the city and catch a glimpse to the north of the huge outline of the Taurus.

Once across the Cestrus, called by the Turks the Ak Su (the white water), the traveller may see on his left the acropolis of Sillyon, the military head-quarters, and then the ruins of Aspendos. He will, doubtless, spare a glance for the aqueduct whose arches and piers, crowned in the spring by the 'storks of Islam', rise above the hovels of Balkiz. He will rest for a moment upon one of the seats of the splendid Roman theatre, perhaps the most imposing of the ancient world, and gaze upon the mouth of the Eurymedon where once an Athenian fleet de-stroyed the fleet of the Great King. Farther east, he will come at length to Side, an ancient Aeolian colony and a port destined to have a notable future in the early centuries of the empire.

The account in Acts does not tell us where St. Paul and his companions landed, and the conjec-tures which have been made concerning the point seem utterly futile. Neither do we know anything about a first stay at Perga, and are only informed that the missionaries pushed on at once to the high-lands without delaying in Pamphylia. Various reasons have been offered to explain this haste and apparent reluctance on the part of the apostle to evangelize the important cities of the Pamphylian plain. Ram-say, in his book *St. Paul the Traveller and the Roman Citizen*,[1] has recalled the illness of the apostle men-tioned in a passage of the Epistle to the Galatians: 'You know', wrote Paul, 'that because of an infirmity

[1] *St. Paul the Traveller and the Roman Citizen*, p. 94 f.

of the flesh I preached the gospel to you the first time' (4.13). May not this infirmity of the flesh which drove Paul to evangelize the vast province of Galatia —if we assume that by this title he was referring to the province of Galatia in its entirety, according to its official designation, and not to the Galatic region bordering on Phrygia, which was to be the object of the second mission[1]—have been some form of malaria, from which his Cilician origin had not rendered the apostle immune, but rather the opposite? On this assumption it is easily understandable that Paul, worn out by his stay in Cyprus, had not been able to withstand the depressing climate of the Pamphylian plain, and had decided to push on to the higher altitudes as quickly as possible.

Pisidian Antioch. We have been reminded by others that the apostle's itineraries were dictated by his desire to visit the Jewish colonies, and that there was a synagogue in Pisidian Antioch. While we willingly admit this, it does not diminish our surprise at Paul's reluctance to evangelize a province which embraced important urban centres, extensively hellenized. Later on, in similar circumstances, the apostle displayed the same reluctance with regard to the province of Asia. It would appear that he did not make it his aim, at least at the outset of his missionary journeys, to convert the Greek or hellenized populations of the Anatolian seaboard, and that his preaching was in the first place addressed to the small cities or even to

[1] See below, p. 34.

the villages of the interior. Perhaps his Cilician origins caused him to find a more congenial audience among the wholly Anatolian populations.

The road from Perga to Pisidian Antioch is long and often difficult, at times even dangerous. Doubtless the imperial police had not yet entirely suppressed the raiding activities of the Isaurian bandits. Our travellers would follow the course of the Cestrus and, after crossing the mountain barrier of the Taurus, would reach Lake Egridir. Until recently a little Orthodox chapel dedicated to Haghio Pavlo reminded believers that the apostle had passed that way. Leaving the Taurus, with its deep valleys and its lakes which at times recall those of the Alps, Paul and Barnabas would emerge upon the lofty, half-desert, plateau which leads to ancient Antioch, the modern Yalovatch.[1] Nothing, indeed, seemed to offer a reason why this small city, buried in the Pisidian plain (Pl. 3), which Augustus had recently created a Roman colony with Italian citizenship, should have been chosen to receive the apostle's message, unless it were, perhaps, the presence of an important Jewish colony. At all events, it was also a market and a road junction: we recall the advantage which Paul took of this situation when, confronted by the invincible hostility of the Jews, he turned to the Gentiles (Acts 13.46). There were numerous conversions among the genuine pagans, whose very isolation rendered them a more fruitful soil for the

[1] Not to be confused with Antioch on the Orontes, a Syrian city.

reception of the new teaching, and now Paul's mission was no longer directed solely to the city dwellers, but embraced the population, mainly rural, of the entire countryside. Jewish pressure seems to have forced the city magistrates to expel the missionaries. Paul and Barnabas fled to Lycaonia, a country in all respects similar to that which they had just left. There were the same desert plateaux, scorching in summer, covered with snow in winter, the same type of population mainly consisting of slightly hellenized nomads. They still spoke, as the narrative of Acts informs us, a Lycaonian dialect. The persistence of these ancient indigenous cults is noteworthy: the votive inscriptions, some of which date from the third or fourth century of our era, speak of a 'Saviour' god, of 'Immortal' gods, and all the cultic variants of the Mother-goddess. The apostles reached Iconium, the future Konia of the Seldjuk sultans. There they found, as at Antioch, an important Jewish colony, no doubt of Cilician extraction, but they addressed their message at once to the Gentiles where again it found a favourable soil. A Church was founded whose renown spread beyond the boundaries of the province. The Acts of Paul and Thekla, an interesting romance of mystic love, composed in Asia during the reign of Marcus Aurelius, named Iconium as the meeting-place of Paul and the lady who was to be the most devoted of his disciples.

The Cities of Lycaonia. A disturbance, instigated by the Jews, forced the apostles into fresh flight. This

time they found asylum in two obscure cities, one
of which was Lystra, on the borders of Lycaonia and
Isauria, and the other Derbe, on the northern slopes
of the Cilician Taurus. The district passed for one
of the most inhospitable in Asia Minor. When Cicero
was proconsul of Cilicia, he could not find sufficiently
opprobrious terms to describe its rustic and un-
lettered inhabitants. The narrative of Acts, moreover, bears vivid witness to Lycaonian gullibility.
When the report spread abroad in Lystra that Paul
had miraculously healed a lame man, 'the multi-
tudes lifted up their voice, saying in the speech of
Lycaonia, The gods are come down to us in the
likeness of men' (Acts 14.11-12). The belief in epi-
phanies of the gods[1] was an essential element in
Lycaonian religion. Barnabas was equated with
Zeus and Paul with Hermes, the god of eloquence,
and the priest of Zeus at once prepared to offer
sacrifice before the temple of Zeus.

The bitter enmity of the Jews, who had come
from Antioch or Iconium, compelled Paul to flee
once again: his flight brought him to Derbe, the
farthest limit of his first journey. There he made a
prolonged stay, in the course of which, as he had
done at Lystra, he addressed his message mainly to
the Gentiles. These young Lycaonian Churches
assumed a hitherto unfamiliar character. The influence of the synagogue upon them faded, and this

---

[1] This is the term used by the ancient religions to indicate divine
appearances.

may be one of the reasons for the interest which the apostle subsequently took in them. A second missionary journey was destined to bring him back to this remote and backward region, where he would be rewarded by the attachment of two of his most devoted companions.

For unknown reasons which have presented an insoluble problem to the commentators, St. Paul did not extend his progress farther east, but turned and retraced his footsteps by the same route which he had followed from the Pamphylian plain to the Lycaonian plateau. He revisited Lystra, Iconium, and Antioch, where he made it his care to introduce some degree of organization into the Churches which he had founded. After a sojourn in Pisidia, he returned to Perga, the starting point of his first Anatolian mission. 'He preached the word in that city', which, a few years earlier, he had merely passed through; he then went on to the neighbouring port of Attaleia (Pl. 4*a*), where he took ship for Seleucia and Antioch on the Orontes.

Although Paul's first Anatolian mission only touched comparatively unimportant districts, yet its results had a far-reaching significance; the gospel had been preached with success to the Gentiles for the first time; Churches had been established beyond the bounds of the Jewish world; in its infancy Christianity had found a welcome in the pagan world. For centuries to come Asia Minor was destined to afford a home to the new religion.

III

THE SECOND MISSION

The narrative of Acts seems to imply that Paul and
Barnabas made a fairly long stay at Antioch. We
learn that the apostles then 'went up' to Jerusalem
to give an account of their work among the Gentiles,
and returned thence to Antioch, accompanied by
Judas and Silas, 'chief men among the brethren'.

'And after some days Paul said to Barnabas, Let
us return now and visit the brethren in every city
wherein we proclaimed the word of the Lord, and
see how they fare. And Barnabas was minded to take
with them John also, who was called Mark. But
Paul thought not good to take with them him who
withdrew from them from Pamphylia, and went not
with them to the work. And there arose a sharp
contention, so that they parted asunder one from
the other, and Barnabas took Mark with him, and
sailed away unto Cyprus; but Paul chose Silas, and
went forth, being commended by the brethren to
the grace of the Lord. And he went through Syria
and Cilicia, confirming the churches' (Acts 14.36-41).

Thus began the second mission, more continental
and more Anatolian, at least at the outset, than the
first. We can see from the map (fig. II) that St.

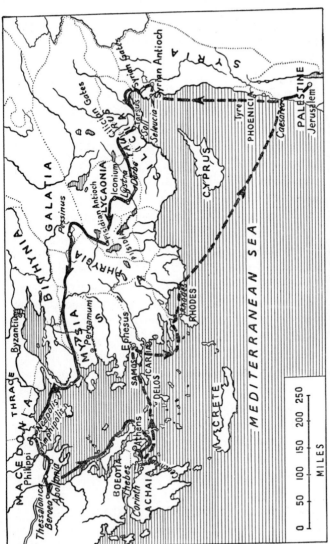

II. ST. PAUL'S SECOND MISSIONARY JOURNEY

Paul, starting from Antioch, where he had made a long stay, and passing through the gorge of the Amanus and 'the Syrian Gates', first of all reached Cilicia, where he had been born, and whither he had retired after his conversion.

New Cilicia. Partly Anatolian, partly Syrian, ancient Cilicia was divided into two districts, a mountainous Cilicia on the east, and a low-lying Cilicia on the west. Ancient authorities agreed in considering Phoenicia as the provenance of the population of Cilicia, which fact they recorded in the tradition that Cilicia had been peopled by the progeny of the hero Cilix, the son of Agenor, the king of Phoenicia. In reality, in spite of its maritime character, Cilicia was very slow in submitting to Greek influence. The coinage of Cilician cities bears witness to the existence of various oriental cults, among others that of a Hercules which is closely akin to his Syrian namesake. It is possible that their kinship with the Phoenicians had endowed the Cilicians with that aptitude for seamanship which made them such formidable pirates. Involved in Alexander's conquest of the Persians, Cilicia was also involved in the fate of his vast empire. She became part of the kingdom of the rulers of Syria, and after the defeat of Antiochus III in 188 B.C. she was included in that part of his dominion which the Romans permitted the conquered king to retain. In the first century B.C., and after the transitory rule of Mithridates, Cilicia became a Roman province.

3. Pisidian Antioch

4 (*a*). Attaleia

4 (*b*). Athens. The Areopagus

As such she was governed by Cicero whose impressions of the district which had come under his rule were in no wise more favourable than his verdict on its neighbour Lycaonia.

Terse as is the narrative of Acts, it is nevertheless probable that Paul and Silas prolonged their stay in Cilicia. Moreover, Paul felt himself at home here. In spite of his trade, he had studied at the schools which made Tarsus the intellectual capital of the province, whereas its neighbour Soli was notorious for the rusticity of its speech. Perhaps he had attended the gymnasium for the young, which stood on the banks of the Cydnus, a river whose icy waters were famous. However, Cilicia was not to be more than a stage on his journey; the Churches of the interior were beckoning him. Hence he left the coastal plain and reached the high plateau by the only passable road which crosses the Taurus, the famous Cilician Gates, through which in the past Alexander had launched his armies for the conquest of the Persian empire, and through which, centuries later, the Crusaders were to pour down upon the Holy Land. The apostle, then, rejoined his churches in Derbe and Lystra. The believers had increased in number. Timothy, who had been only a child at the time of the first mission, had developed into a man of whom the Lycaonian converts spoke in the highest terms. Paul attached him to his person, and, in order not to offend the susceptibilities of the Jews who were living there, circumcised him himself. From Iconium

Paul no doubt moved on to Pisidian Antioch, and it was after they left Antioch that Paul and Silas turned towards Phrygia and Galatia.

'And they went through the region of Phrygia and Galatia, having been forbidden of the Holy Spirit to speak the word in Asia' (Acts 16.6).

The expression 'the Galatic region' seems to have been employed deliberately to denote Galatia in the strict sense of the term, the district lying to the north of Lycaonia, which had been invaded in 278 B.C. by a Celtic migration, and to distinguish this Galatia from the Roman province of that name, which embraced, in addition to the Galatic region, Lycaonia, Pisidia, and Isauria. The eastern part of Phrygia also belonged to it, and it is this eastern Phrygia which is referred to here. Paul, Silas, and Timothy travelled in this direction, 'having been forbidden by the Holy Spirit to preach the word in Asia'. Asia here does not mean the whole of Anatolia: it denotes the proconsular province of western Asia, embracing the most populous and wealthy cities, Ephesus, Miletus, Smyrna, and Pergamum. Paul and Silas, on leaving Cilicia, had crossed the Lycaonian plateau from east to west, and then the Pisidian plateau. They would naturally incline thereupon to follow down the valley of the Maeander towards the western boundary of Anatolia. Instead of pursuing this obvious course, the apostles deliberately turned northwards, and it might be thought that in abandoning for the time being the idea of evangelizing the Greek districts of the Aegean coast, they had acted similarly with regard to Phrygia and Galatia; but a careful perusal of the narrative of Acts militates against this hypothesis. In the course of his third missionary journey St. Paul returned to the Galatic region, and we are told that he passed through this district confirming the disciples. Hence it may be reasonably inferred that he had already founded Churches in the course of his previous visit.

Phrygia and the Galatic region. Phrygia, the next scene of St. Paul's missionary activity, was one of the least hellenized of the Anatolian regions: in earlier times, before the Persian conquest, it had possessed an indigenous civilization to which the Midas legend remains a witness. It was a country of an inclement and continental climate, the home of strange cults. The most famous of these, the cult of Cybele, was noted for the wild orgies of its votaries; but these very orgies had been instrumental in carrying the renown of the Phrygian goddess as far as Rome, where her cult had been the precursor of the invasion of the capital by other oriental cults. In the fifth century another Phrygian god, Sabazios, had reached Athens, and we know with what gibes Demosthenes loaded his opponent Aeschines, taunting him with the possession of a mother who was the priestess of a petty Asiatic god. More nearly contemporary with the apostle was another deity worshipped by the rustic inhabitants of Phrygia, Mên, portrayed on the monuments in 'Phrygian' dress, that is to say, with cap, tunic, cloak, and gaiters, and bearing on his shoulders a lunar crescent. He was a rustic god who protected men and cattle from disease: a whole series of votive inscriptions record his acts of healing or offer prayers for healing. He gave protection against witchcraft, and preserved the graves of the dead from the calamity of violation. At times he extended his protection to a town or an entire family. His cult might be innocent of the mad riotous orgies of the other great Phrygian gods, and he might have gained fewer adherents in foreign countries, yet the universal popularity which he enjoyed in the Asiatic hinterland enabled him to offer a lengthy resistance to the new religion. Into such a country was the apostle's preaching now seeking to penetrate, with varied success, it would seem, for we learn from the Epistle to the Galatians that the new converts were soon led astray by others.

The perplexities of Paul and Silas at the end of their Phrygian mission have given rise to many rash conjectures. When they had reached the north-west corner of Phrygia, no doubt somewhere near Aezani, it was open to the apostles, either to turn north and to reach the Pontic Euxine, that is, the Black Sea, by crossing Bithynia, or to incline westwards and reach the Aegean by way of ancient Mysia. Apparently they first attempted to enter Bithynia, and this move would have been entirely in keeping with their plans. The former kingdom of Prusias, subjugated by Pompey, offered those Anatolian characteristics

which Paul was seeking. It might be thought that
there his message would have found the most favourable conditions for its reception. But, in actuality,
others were destined to found those communities of
whose existence we learn from the letter of Pliny the
Younger, governor of Bithynia at the beginning of
the second century, to the emperor Trajan. Paul,
then, was about to enter the province of Mysia, a
country which, having been incorporated for nearly
two centuries into proconsular Asia, would have
given a visitor the impression of being an almost
entirely Greek country. This province, peopled from
a very early date by Aeolian colonies, had been
allotted to the kings of Syria after the dividing up of
the Macedonian conquests, and had subsequently
passed under the domination of a new Pergamenian
state. Greek was the language of the country, and,
except in the backwoods, the gods generally worshipped were those of the Greek pantheon.

Hence it was a somewhat unfamiliar country
through which the missionaries passed before they
reached the harbour of Troad Alexandria on the
Aegean sea. Here Paul's famous vision occurred:
'There was a man of Macedonia standing, beseech-
ing him, and saying, Come over into Macedonia,
and help us' (Acts 16.9). The editor, who from this
point uses the first person plural, continues: 'And
when he had seen the vision, straightway we sought
to go forth into Macedonia, concluding that God
had called us for to preach the gospel unto them.'

However we may interpret the meaning of the incident, it is impossible to minimize the importance of the decision thus taken. It is true that the departure from Troas has not the significance of the departure from Antioch. The evangelization of heathen lands was no longer a novelty, the decisive step had been taken when Paul and Barnabas embarked for Cyprus and Pamphylia. Paul's latest decision was of a different character. Henceforth he was leaving Anatolia behind. When he crossed over into Macedonia he was entering an entirely different kind of province, not only more civilized than the country of the Galatians or the Phrygians, but also, in the Roman colony of Philippi, revealing to him that vast world of which he had only gained glimpses as he passed through the colonies of Pisidian Antioch or Troad Alexandria.

Paul and his companions put in for a night at Samothrace, but did not take the opportunity of preaching the gospel in this island, famous for its cult of the Cabiri, those strange deities to be met with in the country about Boeotian Thebes; next day the travellers continued their voyage and the same evening reached the port of Neapolis on the coast of Thrace, after a sea journey which seems to have been remarkably rapid. What was then called the province of Macedonia actually consisted of parts of Thrace formerly colonized by the Greeks, then, in the fourth century B.C., annexed by the Macedonian kingdom, and finally, two centuries later, incorporated into the Roman empire. These countries, like the districts of Asia Minor through which Paul had just passed, were resistant to Hellenism in the strict sense. To an even greater degree than Phrygia, to which she was linked by ethnic ties as yet not fully understood, Thrace, too, was the cradle of an orgiastic cult. Just as the lofty plateaux of Phrygia are the home of Cybele, so the summits of Pangeia, the mountain mass which dominates both the valley of the Strymon and the plain of Philippi, have given birth to the cult of Dionysus. The Thracian Dionysus was an agrarian deity, who was believed by the indigenous inhabitants to frequent the mountains with a train of votaries whom he inebriated with an ecstasy akin to madness. Doubtless at the time when St. Paul and his companions landed at Neapolis and beheld for the first time the peaks of the frowning mass of Pangeia outlined against the sunset, the cult of Dionysus had already broken its ancient bounds and spread through the Greek world, rudely jostling the gods of the traditional pantheon, invading the Delphic oracle, and thrusting in among the Eleusinian deities. Nonetheless, we are bound to remark on the apostle's strange preference for presenting his message to a people already under the spell of an ecstatic religion, rather than to the intellectual and moral idealism of Athenian philosophers.

Philippi. From Neapolis the apostle followed the Via Egnatia, an important Roman trunk road

connecting Dyrrachium (Durazzo) on the Adriatic
with the Thracian coast. A journey of three or four
hours brought him to Philippi, a city, which, if not
founded, was at least strongly re-fortified by Philip
of Macedon in 356 B.C. During three centuries the
fortunes of this little city had been bound up with
those of the kingdom of its founder, but in 42 B.C.
an interruption to its development occurred. The
leaders of the republican cause, Brutus and Cassius,
met the united forces of Antony and Octavian in a
decisive battle. The republicans suffered a total defeat, and the two leaders committed suicide, while
the conquerors proceeded to re-partition the empire,
and settled some of their troops, discharged after
the battle, in Philippi itself. These veterans became
the nucleus of an important Roman colony, and the
insignificant little market town which they occupied
underwent a consequent transformation. Public
buildings and private houses sprang up along the
Via Egnatia, which naturally became the Decu-
manus Maximus of the city. The centre of the city
was occupied by the Forum, an open square of about
fifty by one hundred metres, paved with great marble
blocks and surrounded by porticos or temples. To
the east of the Forum rose the theatre, whose tiers
of seats long escaped destruction.

St. Paul's first preoccupation was to get into touch
with the Jewish minority inhabiting this Roman city.
This he did by attending the Jewish *proseuché* or
synagogue which, according to the narrative of Acts,

was by the river-side. It has been suggested that this river was the Gangites which flows some distance from the city, but the circumstances would be better suited by something nearer the city, and it seems more probable that the Jews had their *proseuché* in the garden of one of their own houses near the stream to which the narrative refers. The details of his mission and the troubles which he encountered at Philippi, as elsewhere, may be found in all the lives of the apostle. Here only one detail need be enlarged upon, namely the form which the opposition to the apostle took in Philippi. Contrary to the usual course of events related in Acts, it was not the Jews who stirred up hostile activities, as at Pisidian Antioch, Lystra, and later on at Corinth; but it was the Romans who denounced Paul and Silas as Jews who were engaged in illegal propaganda, illegal because it was addressed to Romans. The incident gives us extremely interesting information concerning the attitude of the Roman authorities with regard to Christian preaching, at a time when it was still impossible to distinguish it from Judaism.[1]

After leaving Philippi, Paul and Silas followed the Egnatian road in the direction of Amphipolis, the provincial capital, an hour's distance from the mouth of the Strymon. They do not seem to have tarried in this entirely Greek city, but went straight on to Apollonia, whence they arrived at Thessalonica at the head of its gulf. Here the apostles found

Cf. P. Lemerle, *Philippes . . . à l'époque chrétienne*, p. 34.

themselves in a large city, one of the busiest trading ports of the Mediterranean. They found a synagogue there, and Paul, as was his wont, took the opportunity to preach in it. The Church which resulted from his activity became a model to which St. Paul later on was proud to point; however, once more the Jews stirred up trouble and raised a hostile crowd.

'The brethren immediately sent away Paul and Silas by night unto Beroea.' Beroea was a fair-sized town, off the main roads. Here he met with a better reception from the Jewish colony than at Thessalonica, and had full liberty to preach the gospel in the synagogue until the Jews from Thessalonica again stirred up trouble for the apostles. Since Macedonia was getting too hot to hold him, Paul made for the nearest port and sailed for Athens. So ended the Macedonian mission. It proved to be one of the most fruitful of all Paul's enterprises, and, in any case, it is the one about which we are most fully informed. The next question was whether, with Judaism as its forerunner, Christianity was to gain a footing in the very heart of ancient Greece.

Athens. Although the narrative of Acts does not give us precise information on the point, it is natural to suppose that Paul travelled from Macedonia to Athens by sea. It was certainly the easiest way. Embarking at Methone or Alorus, Paul would first skirt Olympus whose peaks, often veiled by mists, were the dwelling-place of Zeus and the great gods.

Then, rounding the point of Pelion, he would probably enter the narrow channel which separates Euboea from the mainland. After a voyage of four or five days, having avoided the reefs off Cape Sunium, surmounted by the temple of Poseidon, the ship which bore Paul and his Beroean converts would finally make harbour at the Piraeus or Phalerum.

In the middle of the first century A.D., ancient Greece, then the province of Achaia, had never recovered from the blows inflicted on her during the unceasing wars of the previous centuries. Famous cities like Thebes or Argos, with an illustrious history, had become poverty-stricken villages, the fields lay waste, a spectacle of ruin and desolation shocking to all who travelled their roads or sought for traces of their golden age. Athens and Corinth alone, in this wretched country, still preserved the semblance of great cities.

'Life in Athens is merely the leisured existence of a provincial university city, the home of art treasures, which enjoys in a calm and safe monotony the prestige of its illustrious past, and of its status as a free city, at least in name.'[1] Although, like the rest of Greece, it had been plundered by Roman governors, the city of Pallas could still present to the traveller the most amazing spectacle which the ancient world had to offer. The monuments of the Acropolis, still unharmed, rose in the midst of an infinite profusion of pillars and altars of every kind. While he awaited

[1] Graindor, *Athènes de Tibère à Trajan*, p. 1.

Silas and Timothy, whom he had instructed to join
him as quickly as possible, Paul was free to explore
the city, to climb the slopes of the sacred rock, and
to wander under the shadow of the Parthenon. What
must this Cilician Jew have felt as he gazed on those
sculptured pediments depicting the ancient legends
of Attica, the birth of Athene, the strife between
Poseidon and Athene for the possession of the future
city? Without wishing to emulate the well-known
sentimental apostrophe of Renan: 'O chaste and
lovely forms, true gods and goddesses, tremble! The
iconoclast is here. The doom has been uttered: You
are idols . . .', we must acknowledge that, perhaps
for the first time, the apostle felt himself an alien
confronted by a world which did not understand
him, and which he too could never understand.

Both the Athenian religion and the eschatological
beliefs which accompanied it presented a formidable
obstacle to Paul's preaching. The very ancient agrarian mysteries celebrated in September in the Tele-
sterion of Eleusis in honour of Demeter, Core,
Dionysus, and Triptolemus continued to attract
crowds of votaries. Even the emperors, headed by
Augustus, submitted to the rites of initiation.
Claudius entertained the idea of transferring the
ceremonies to Rome; Nero, murderer of his mother,
on the occasion of his visit to Greece, dared not
appear at Eleusis, being aware that before the per-
formance of every ritual the Eleusinian hierophant
bade all profane persons and criminals withdraw.

But it was the essential Greek spirit, more than all the Eleusinian mysteries, more than the poetic procession of those ancient chthonic deities whose cult still retained its vitality at the beginning of the imperial age, that was immune to Paul's message. The characteristic feature of the religion of bygone Greece was its lack of any sense of the infinite; to no people has mysticism ever seemed less congenial; Greek philosophic speculation had always been interested in the problem of the immortality of the soul, but it rejected indignantly the doctrine of the resurrection.

While awaiting the arrival of Silas and Timothy, Paul 'reasoned in the synagogue with the Jews and the devout persons, and in the marketplace every day with them that met with him. And certain also of the Epicurean and Stoic philosophers encountered him. And some said, What would this babbler say? other some, He seemeth to be a setter forth of strange gods: because he preached Jesus and the resurrection. And they took hold of him, and brought him unto the Areopagus, saying, May we know what this new teaching is, which is spoken by thee? For thou bringest certain strange things to our ears: we would know therefore what these things mean' (17.17-20).

The reason why Paul was brought before the tribunal of the Areopagus (Pl. 6*b*) was that he was charged with proselytism on behalf of foreign deities, and the Stoic and Epicurean philosophers were only exercising a right accorded to them by Athenian law, of bringing offenders taken in the act of committing a crime, before the competent authorities. The council sitting on the Areopagus was a very ancient Athenian institution, whose powers had gradually diminished as democracy developed. Its function, according to Aristotle, was to guard the laws; originally it was responsible for the major and most important share of the government, and it had absolute power to deal with breaches of public order by fines or corporal punishments. Weakened by the democratic reforms of Cleisthenes at the close of the sixth century, the Areopagus recovered, after the Persian wars, its executive power, but soon its decay became accelerated. In the fourth century its functions were limited to being merely a tribunal empowered to deal with premeditated murder and charges of impiety. From the narrative of Acts we learn that it still exercised this function in the Roman period. It is still a matter of dispute whether St. Paul was conducted to Mars Hill on the west slope of the Acropolis, the traditional meeting place of the Areopagus, or whether his examination took place in the royal portico of the Agora where the tribunal sometimes assembled during the imperial period. It should be observed, moreover, that Paul was not brought before the Areopagus to be judged, but rather that the Areopagites might be informed concerning the precise nature of his teaching; hence the Areopagus assumed the function of a court of enquiry for the nonce.

From the speech delivered by the apostle we may select for discussion his reference to 'the unknown

[46]

god' which served as his text. In reality, no well-attested example, either in literary texts, or in inscriptions, of a similar dedication in the singular, is known, whereas several instances of the plural occur. The traveller Pausanias, in the second century B.C., visited the sites of ancient Greece, and has left a frequently detailed description of them. Among the shrines of the harbour of Munychia, near the Piraeus, he mentions the altars of 'unknown' gods. The same Pausanias refers to a similar monument at Olympus, near the great altar of Olympian Zeus. Such dedications are significant: the Greeks erected altars to 'unknown gods' in order to ensure that no deity was omitted from their worship, whose wrath might be incurred by such omission. Another point in the speech calls for notice, the apostle's quotation from the *Phenomena* of the poet Aratus.[1] This poet of the third century B.C., who belonged to the school of Alexandria and spent part of his life at the court of Antigonus Gonatas, king of Macedon, came from Soli in Cilicia. Doubtless in the schools of Tarsus where St. Paul had studied in his youth, the works of a poet who was rightly regarded as a local worthy were studied with pride. It is hardly surprising, then, that when the apostle attempted to address the Athenians in their own tongue, he should recall a quotation from this poet. Biblical criticism has often questioned the authenticity of St. Paul's speech, at least in the form in which it has been transmitted

[1] Aratus, *Phenomena*, 5: 'We also are his offspring.'

to us in the text of Acts. I should, however, be inclined to regard this quotation from Aratus as an actual reminiscence of the apostle's discourse, carrying with it a guarantee of its authenticity.

We know that St. Paul's address found little response. The very absurdity of the doctrine rendered it harmless, and made it unnecessary to expel its promulgator; hence the apostle benefited by the suspension of his case. He abandoned the attempt, however, and, without waiting for Silas and Timothy to arrive, he left the city of Pallas for Corinth where his preaching was destined to have a very different success.

Corinth. Corinth (Pl. 5) presented a much more promising field than Athens. The old Greek city had been destroyed by Mummius in 146 B.C., after a most cruel siege, and little was left save the massive columns of the ancient temple as reminder of the great commercial city which, several centuries earlier, had flooded the whole Mediterranean basin with the products of its industries. It was rebuilt in 44 B.C. by Julius Caesar, who had made it an important Roman colony with a population consisting mainly of freedmen, and since 27 B.C. it had been the capital of the province of Achaia. Notorious for its licentiousness, the new Corinth was a cosmopolitan city which long remained alien to Greece. The mixed character of its population, its luxury, and its mercantile activity might make it comparable with one of the great modern Mediterranean ports, such as Alexandria or Marseilles, or even more

5. Corinth from the Acrocorinthus

appropriately with the Smyrna of the old Ottoman empire.

Timothy and, no doubt, Silas, whom St. Paul had summoned after his arrival at Athens, rejoined him at Corinth, and the three companions remained together during a prolonged sojourn in the city. We are justified in speaking of St. Paul's long and concentrated efforts here as a Corinthian ministry. The Epistles to the Corinthians give us some insight into the many-sided nature of a ministry whose duration we know to have been eighteen months. At the outset, the apostle's preaching was, as usual, addressed to Jews, but soon his message was exclusively directed to Gentiles. Jewish opposition took the form of an appeal to the Roman government, and incidentally to the governor of the province, the proconsul Gallio. Marcus Annaeus Novatus was the son of the rhetorician Marcus Annaeus Seneca, and the elder brother of Seneca the philosopher. Having been adopted by the rhetorician L. Junius Gallio, he assumed the name of his adoptive father. He was a charming and cultured person, and it is probable that his distinguished Greek culture may have been the reason why Claudius chose him to administer Achaia. By a happy chance we know the date of his proconsulate: Gallio is mentioned in an inscription at Delphi dated A.D. 51-2. Such was the typical representative of Greco-Roman culture into whose presence the Jews of the synagogue dragged St. Paul, but the proconsul was uninterested in 'a discussion of doctrine', and Paul escaped the hostile intentions of his opponents on this occasion.

We learn from the narrative of Acts that Paul stayed on some time at Corinth, carrying on his apostolic ministry. It was at this time that he wrote the first of his letters to the Churches which he had founded. However, after an absence of nearly three years, he felt the need of revisiting the churches of Syria, and of getting into touch again with the Church at Jerusalem. 'He took his leave of the brethren, and sailed thence for Syria, and with him Priscilla and Aquila; having shorn his head in Cenchreae, for he had a vow' (18.18). The apostle had decided to keep the coming feast in Jerusalem, and had bound himself by a vow in order to give his decision a religious sanction. Paul and his companions, then, will have taken ship at Cenchreae on the Saronic gulf, a port of embarkation for east-bound voyages. They would first have skirted the shores of Megara and Attica, their ship would then have threaded its way through the Cyclades without ever losing sight of land. Once out at sea, the travellers may have passed Apollo's sacred isle, rising gradually above the ruins heaped up by the soldiers of Mithridates in the previous century; the next stage would bring them to Samos, hard by the Asiatic coast, and finally they would reach Ephesus, the provincial capital. But Paul, though he left Aquila and Priscilla there, did not linger in this city which, later, was to become the scene of his ministry.

IV

THE THIRD MISSIONARY JOURNEY

Much research has been devoted to the beginnings of the third missionary journey, the sojourn of St. Paul at Antioch, his dispute with St. Peter, the apostle of the circumcision, and with the emissaries of James, the head of the Jerusalem Church. In pursuance of the course which we have adopted, we shall adhere closely to the text of Acts:

The Dispute at Antioch. 'He went up and saluted the church (at Jerusalem), and went down to Antioch. And having spent some time there, he departed, and went through the region of Galatia and Phrygia in order, stablishing all the disciples' (18.22-3).

Once again Antioch is the starting point of a missionary journey, the indispensable link between Jerusalem and the Gentile world. Great changes had taken place since the day when Paul and Barnabas left Antioch for Cyprus and Pamphylia. Then everything was uncertain. No one could foresee how far Paul's preaching would succeed, or where he would find a receptive soil. Would it be among the Greeks, the peoples of Asia Minor, or the Roman colonies? All these questions the apostle was now in a position to answer in some measure. In the course of this new journey, it would not be so much a matter of gaining fresh territory, except in the case of the Ephesian ministry, as of confirming, teaching, and restoring the Churches which had already experienced the grace of God. For the apostle had received disquieting news of the Churches which he had founded in the course of his great missionary venture in Asia Minor. His opponents had taken upon them to evangelize his new converts with a gospel that was not his, and apparently with success. St. Paul had countered this rival mission with a passionate letter written perhaps from Antioch. But after having despatched the letter, he was doubtless moved with the desire to temper its effect, or at least to bring his converts once more under the influence of his oral instruction. The new Anatolian mission began like the previous one. With unwearied missionary zeal the apostle revisited in turn the cities of Cilicia, Lycaonia, and Pisidia. It may have been on this occasion that Gaius of Derbe, of whom we shall hear later, was added to the little group of St. Paul's faithful followers. At this point the narrative of Acts is very condensed, but it may be inferred from the reference to the Galatic region and Phrygia that after St. Paul had reached Pisidia, he pursued the same course as on his second journey, and avoiding the direct approach to Ephesus, he turned towards the central provinces of Asia Minor. Doubtless he made a prolonged stay there, for after the editor

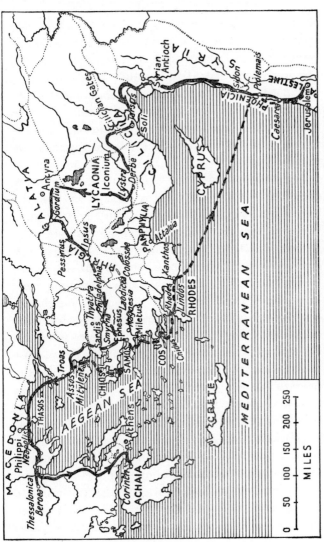

III. ST. PAUL'S THIRD MISSIONARY JOURNEY

of Acts had briefly referred to the presence of Apollos at Ephesus, he goes on to inform us that St. Paul came down to Ephesus after having passed through 'the upper country'. This can only be the plateaux of Phrygia and Galatia, those arid and miserable steppes, inhabited by the worshippers of Cybele or of Mên, the folk who carved those curious funerary monuments in the shape of doors which puzzle the modern traveller.

Phrygia and Galatia. It would be interesting to know the route by which the apostles came down from the lofty plateaux into Proconsular Asia. Perhaps they followed the road which led from Ancyra (the modern Ankara), bringing them to Ephesus by way of Gordium, Pessinus, Ipsus, and Sardis. It will be remembered that Sardis, the ancient capital of the kingdom of Lydia, is one of the seven Churches of the Apocalypse, and it is attractive to connect the founding of that Church with a possible visit of St. Paul; however, the other Churches of the Apocalypse might claim the same distinction. Philadelphia, the modern Alashēhir, an insignificant little town at the foot of Mount Tmolus, lies to the south-east of Sardis; farther east, on a tributary of the Maeander, stands Laodicea in the Lycus valley; founded in the third century B.C. by Antiochus II, king of Syria, it was destined to become an important trading centre on the main route leading from Proconsular Asia to Cilicia and Syria. Although they do not occur in the Apocalypse, mention may be made of two neighbouring Churches: Colossae, the commercial rival of Laodicea, distinguished as the recipient of an apostolic letter, dated from Rome, and Hierapolis, whose Church is greeted by St. Paul in his Epistle to the Colossians.

Leaving the group of Churches in the Lycus valley and moving north-west from Sardis, we come to Thyatira, the white city, lying in a wide valley watered by a tributary of the Hermus; here, in earlier times, the Seleucid kings had settled a colony of their veterans. Passing on westwards we come to Pergamos in the valley of the Caicus, a city with an interesting history. At the beginning of the third century B.C. the Thracian ruler Lysimachus had stored his treasures in one of his strongholds in north-west Asia Minor, and had placed a certain Paphlagonian named Philetairos in charge of it. After Lysimachus had put to death his own son Agathocles, the friend of Philetairos, the Paphlagonian offered his services to Seleucus and thus enabled the king of Syria to conquer Lysimachus. After the departure of Seleucus, Philetairos considered himself independent, and bequeathed the city and its treasures to his adopted son Eumenes. This was the beginning of a prosperous period for Pergamum, which reached its height in the second century. Eumenes I· was succeeded by Attalus I, Eumenes II, Attalus II, and finally by Attalus III, who, in 133 B.C., bequeathed his kingdom and his treasures to the Romans. The second-rate fortress of

Lysimachus had become a splendid city. The ascending terraces of its acropolis were graced by magnificent buildings, the altar of Zeus, the temple of Athene, the palace of Eumenes, and the gymnasia; at the foot of the acropolis, whose frowning battlements commanded the Selinus and the Cetius, lay the city itself, where today may be seen the picturesque houses of Bergama; finally, outside the walls, stood a shrine of Aesculapius, god of healing, a shrine which became a surprisingly fashionable resort during the Roman period.

Farther south, Smyrna, the second of the Churches mentioned in the Apocalypse, might have attracted St. Paul's attention for more reasons than one. Antigonus, one of Alexander's successors, had intentionally abandoned the site of the ancient city which had been destroyed in the sixth century B.C., and had built a new city at the foot of the Pagus, at the beginning of the Hellenistic period. Unmatched in situation, skilfully laid out, and embellished with graceful colonnades, Smyrna, according to the ancient geographer Strabo, was the finest city of Roman Asia.

Hence each of the cities just named may have been a possible halting-place on the road from the high plateau to Ephesus, but Ephesus was to be the scene of the apostle's activity for the next three years.

Ephesus. Ephesus, like many of the ports of Asia Minor, was situated at the head of an inlet near the mouth of the Cayster, and was left high and dry as the inlet was filled up by the alluvial deposit of the river. At the time of St. Paul's sojourn there, the sea had long ago receded from the ancient acropolis dominating the plain of which Homer had sung: 'As the myriad flocks of feathered fowl, geese, cranes, or long-necked swans, may be seen in the Asian plain, on both banks of the Cayster, flying hither and thither with proudly beating wings, and settling one after the other, with resounding cries from the whole flock' (*Iliad*, II, pp. 459 ff.). Nevertheless, at the foot of this acropolis still stood intact the great temple of Artemis which had been built to replace the ancient temple destroyed by fire in 356 B.C., the very night of Alexander's birth. This temple, which was included among the seven wonders of the world for the wealth of its sculptures and the grace of its proportions, was dedicated to a local mother-goddess, ruling over the marshes of the Cayster, whom the Greek colonists of the eighth century B.C. had identified with their own Artemis. Later legends, edited, no doubt, by the priests of the temple, had it that the goddess, Apollo's sister and Leda's daughter, had been born near by at Ortygia. The fame of this Artemis quickly spread beyond the plain of the Cayster. Crowds of pilgrims flocked thither from all parts of the Greek world and Asia Minor. An industry engaged in the manufacture of votive objects which the worshippers might offer to their goddess, had grown up around the temple. When Christianity triumphed over the ancient pagan cults about the third or fourth century A.D., the temple of Artemis was partly destroyed, and the marsh, no longer drained by the care of a living civilization, encroached upon the ancient site. Masses of earth accumulated upon the ruins. Meanwhile the Byzantines had erected on the hill a magnificent basilica dedicated to St. John the Divine (Pl. 6). In its turn this basilica was destroyed by the Seldjuk Turks. Then victorious Islam built a splendid mosque on the slopes of the same hill, and this, too, neglected, is today half ruined. Few sites present so perfect a picture of inevitable decay as the hill of Ayasoluk.[1]

When King Lysimachus, at the beginning of the Hellenistic period, decided to rebuild the city and restore it to its pristine greatness, he selected a site much further west, and his first act was to provide the new city with an easily accessible harbour. A great city came into being, laid out after the usual pattern of Hellenistic cities, and when the Romans created the province of Asia, they chose Ephesus for the proconsular residence. Such was the city, destined to be, with Jerusalem and Antioch, the third capital of the Christian world (Pl. 7a). It has frequently been observed that in its early stages Christianity showed a preference for the great trading centres, whose character was less stereotyped and possessed

---

[1] The state of the ruins is a striking illustration of the ancient Sibylline prediction, preserved by Clement of Alexandria, *Protrept.* II, IV, 50: 'Overturned, Ephesus shall mourn, weeping on the slopes of her Acropolis and seeking in vain for her temple which shall have no more worshippers.'

fewer local traditions. Perhaps to an even greater degree than Corinth and Antioch, Ephesus, as a city of traders and seafarers, and also of courtesans and rakes, swarmed with magicians, soothsayers, and purveyors of charms, all products and supporters of a gross superstition which had gradually replaced the ancient cults. When Paul arrived in Ephesus in A.D. 52 or 53 he found Aquila and Priscilla, who had been his companions at Corinth, already there; he settled down with them, no doubt in the suburbs of the city between Mount Prium and the hill Ayasoluk. All the accounts tell of the conflicts which Paul experienced with the Jewish exorcists, or with Demetrius the silversmith, and special emphasis may be laid here on the Ephesian period as one of wide diffusion of the Pauline message: 'All they which dwelt in Asia heard the word of the Lord, both Jews and Greeks' (19.10).

Many Churches sprang up in the greater part of western Asia Minor of which Paul may be said to have been the founder, either directly or indirectly.

Macedonia and Corinth. In the belief that his ministry here was finished, Paul made plans for the future; first he would go to Jerusalem after a visit to Macedonia and Achaia, and then he would travel to Rome. So he sent two of his assistants, Timothy and Erastus, to Macedonia, while he himself stayed a little longer in Ephesus; it is at this juncture that the narrative of Acts places the silversmiths' riot. After this incident, 'Paul . . . took leave of the disciples and departed for to go into Macedonia. And when he had gone through those parts, and had given them much exhortation, he came into Greece . . . and spent three months there' (20.1-3).

While the narrative of Acts is silent as to the reasons which led Paul to undertake this fresh journey to Macedonia and Achaia, and gives us little information about the journey itself, various passages in the Epistles are more enlightening. We learn that the chief purpose of the proposed journey to Jerusalem was to carry thither the proceeds of the collections made by the Churches which the apostle had founded. In addition, the first Epistle to the Corinthians (16.5-8) has an explicit reference to a visit of the apostle to Corinth which can neither have been the long ministry during 50-51, nor the visit which the apostle proposed to make according to the passage which has just been quoted: 'But with you it may be I shall abide, or even winter, that ye may set me forward on my journey whithersoever I go. For I do not wish to see you now by the way; for I hope to tarry awhile with you, if the Lord permit. But I will tarry at Ephesus until Pentecost. . . .'

We should place St. Paul's short visit to the Corinthians about the middle or end of 55, on which occasion he merely went there and back from Ephesus, the scene of his missionary activity during these decisive years.

The journey from Corinth to Jerusalem. From a passage in the second Epistle to the Corinthians we gather information about the last journey to Macedonia. St. Paul took ship, as on the first occasion, from Troad Alexandria, in which port, no doubt, he stayed some time and preached the gospel. This time we are told nothing about the apostle's itinerary; we only hear that on his arrival in Macedonia he met with nothing but difficulties: 'Without were fightings, within were fears' (II Cor. 7.6). Perhaps he stayed at Philippi as on his first journey, if we may assume that Philippi was the headquarters of missionary activity in Macedonia. At all events the apostle went on from thence to Corinth, where he stayed three months, as we learn from the Epistles but not from Acts, which only refers to a sojourn in Greece. St. Paul was accompanied by the delegates from Macedonia and Asia. As he was preparing to embark for Syria, no doubt from Cenchreae, the Jews laid an ambush for him, so he decided to travel overland, that is, through central Greece and Macedonia (Acts 20.3-4).

The Church in Athens was so negligible that either St. Paul did not think it worth while to pay it a visit, or the editor of Acts did not trouble to mention the visit. No details are available concerning the third Macedonian journey, except the fact that the delegates went ahead of Paul to Troad Alexandria, while the apostle and that member of his company who uses the pronoun 'we' in his account, kept Passover at Philippi, and did not rejoin their companions until after the days of unleavened bread. This time the voyage to Troas took five days. There St. Paul found the rest of his party. After a brief stay with the disciples, during which the episode of Eutychus occurred, he resumed his journey to Jerusalem where he hoped to arrive in time for Pentecost. From this point onward, as in the case of the first Macedonian mission, the narrative is remarkably detailed, and the stages of the journey can be followed on the map.

For unspecified reasons, perhaps to avoid a particularly disagreeable sea journey, Paul travelled by land to the little port of Assos on the south coast of the Troad. This very ancient city, in ancient times the site of a fine temple, had been robbed of its commercial importance by Alexandria, but it served as a convenient harbour for ships employed in the coasting trade. From Assos St. Paul's ship by-passed the gulf of Adramyttium and set its course for the important island of Mytilene (Pl. 7*b*), following the route between the mainland and the island which is still followed by the regular steam-boat service between Stambul and Smyrna. From Mytilene, Chios, the birthplace of Homer, was reached in a day's sail. The next day, crossing the route formerly followed by St. Paul from Corinth to Ephesus, the travellers reached Samos, facing Mount Mycale, the last peak of the range which separates the valley of the Cayster from that of the Maeander. One of the manuscripts of Acts seems to suggest that instead of anchoring at Samos, St. Paul's ship watered on the coast of Anatolia near Cape Trogila, and before the

Greeks left Asia Minor in 1923 one of the creeks of Mycale still bore the name of 'St. Paul's Harbour'. The next day St. Paul and his companions reached Miletus (Pl. 8*a*).

It would be interesting to know whether this was the apostle's first visit to this extremely important city, the capital of Ionia in the early period, whose revolt in 497 B.C. against the rule of Darius had been ruthlessly suppressed. The fall of the Persian empire before Alexander's onslaught had been for Miletus, as for the other cities of western Anatolia, the opportunity for a resurgence of prosperity. Miletus, situated at the head of the Latmian gulf, now filled up by the alluvial deposit of the Maeander, was advantageously placed for the export of the produce of her fertile hinterland. About fourteen miles farther south, the oracle of Didymean Apollo, overlooking the sea, attracted the crowds of those who wished to consult it. To replace the ancient temple, destroyed by Darius, the Milesians had determined, in the third century B.C., to erect a new one which should surpass all the Asiatic temples in magnificence, but when Paul landed at Miletus it had not yet been completed.

However, in spite of its advantageous commercial situation and the prestige of the shrine of Didymus, Miletus had never recovered the pre-eminence which it possessed before the Persian invasion, and, as we have seen, it was Ephesus which had the honour of being the residence of the proconsul.

Although we do not hear, either in the Epistles or in the Apocalypse, of a Church in Miletus, it would be strange if this city, only a few miles from Ephesus, should never have heard the apostle's message during his prolonged stay in Asia. If he had visited it, it would explain why St. Paul, instead of continuing his journey unbroken as he had hitherto done since leaving Troas, chose to stay a few days at Miletus, and to make contact with his friends in Ephesus. Having summoned the elders of that Church, he made a speech to them in which he summed up the results of his apostolic activity and bade farewell to Asia.

Attended to their ship by the Ephesian elders, St. Paul and his companions resumed their journey. Avoiding, it would seem, the Gulf of Iasus which breaks the Carian coast, their ship, with the help of a favourable wind, reached Cos opposite the peninsula of Halicarnassus, in a day's sail; but the travellers made no long stay in this prosperous island, famous for its shrine of Aesculapius, and whose houses possess some of the most beautiful mosaics in the Greek Orient. The next day they sailed on to the south-east, rounded Cape Triopium and the peninsula of Cnidus, and landed at the capital of the important island of Rhodes, opposite the coast of Anatolia. Rhodes was the diminished capital of a republic which had long been independent. During the Hellenistic period it had maintained its rule over southern Caria and the Lycian

7 (a). Ephesus. Church of the Council

7 (b). Mytilene

8 (*a*). The Agora of Miletus, flooded by the Maeander

8 (*b*). Andriake-Myra

peninsula. It still remained one of the great commercial cities of the eastern Mediterranean, and thus continued to play the role which had belonged to it since the beginnings of Greek civilization. Here, moreover, it is very likely that the Christian gospel had found an entry before the coming of the apostle, but for this there is no documentary evidence. According to a tradition which still survives, the apostle did not land at Rhodes, but at a spot on the east coast of the island, about thirty miles farther south; at the foot of the acropolis of Lindus, whither for many centuries pilgrims resorted to worship Athene Lindia, there is still shown as St. Paul's landing-place, a little inlet with quiet waters. There is no better ground for accepting this tradition than there is for attaching any importance to the trivial building which the guides to Ephesus call 'St. Paul's prison', nor again to that other 'Harbour of St. Paul' which we have already mentioned as located at the foot of Mount Mycale, nor finally to the Greek church of Haghio Pavlo which Sir William Ramsay found in the Pisidian mountains at the end of last century. None the less the persistence of such traditions is interesting as bearing witness, as do also the apocryphal Acts, to the importance which Christian hagiography attached to the journeys of the great apostle.

From Rhodes St. Paul's ship set a course for the Anatolian coast and watered at Patara in Lycia, not far from the mouth of the Xanthus. It seems that this was the first time that the apostle set foot on Lycian soil, although the inhabitants of this strange and only slightly hellenized country possessed, as much as any other Asiatic people, those characteristics which might have attracted him. A people of unknown origin, speaking a language which has not yet been deciphered, the Lycians had lived for centuries on the outskirts of the Greek world, although Homer lists them among the allies of the Trojans. Resisting the inroads of Greek civilization, they had preserved up to the time of Alexander's conquests their cults and their very curious funerary monuments. During the centuries of Greek dominance they were exposed to various foreign influences, especially to that of the Lagid kings of Alexandria, and to that of their Rhodian rivals; in the year A.D. 43 they became part of the Roman empire. During the period of the Roman empire, Patara and Myra, of which we shall have more to say when we follow in the apostle's footsteps towards the west, alone among the ancient Lycian cities possessed any real importance.

Originally Patara was an unimportant market town, built round a shrine of Apollo which, according to Herodotus, rivalled those of Babylon and Egyptian Thebes; under Roman rule it became an important port, and, in the second century A.D., the emperor Hadrian decided to build there, as well as at Myra, the granaries which were to provision his fleets in the eastern Mediterranean. Its forests were one of the principal resources of Lycia, and thither for centuries the Egyptians, and to a lesser degree the Syrians, resorted for the timber which their own countries lacked. (The custom persisted until the middle ages: the Arab fleet in Egypt was accustomed to get the logs for its masts from the Lycian coasts, and even today it is not uncommon to find Egyptian ships in the little port of Fethiye, the ancient Telmessus.) It is most likely that Paul and his companions availed themselves of some such opportunity to leave the coasting vessel which had brought them from Troas to Patara, and to embark on a Phoenician ship sailing direct for Tyre, 'For there the ship was to unlade her burden' (21.3).

Rounding the western coast of Cyprus and passing Paphos where he had once embarked for Pamphylia, after a voyage of six or seven days Paul reached the Phoenician port of Tyre, where there was a Christian Church going back to the earliest days of the mission. Paul was warmly welcomed by the disciples and stayed with them while the ship discharged its cargo. He then continued his journey by sea as far as Ptolemais, then on to Caesarea, the starting point of the road to Jerusalem.

V

ST. PAUL'S JOURNEY AS A PRISONER

The book of Acts has preserved the account of St. Paul's last voyage which was to take him to Caesarea, Myra, Lasea, Malta, and Puteoli. It is only the first part of this journey which concerns us here. Placed with a number of other prisoners in the charge of a centurion named Julius, Paul sailed in a ship of Adramyttium which returned to its port of origin, hugging the shore, a precaution made necessary by the lateness of the sailing season. From this point the narrator uses the first person plural, as in the two previous passages of Acts, and, as in them, furnishes us with such exact details that we can follow the stages of the journey on the map (fig. IV), as we did in the case of the journey from Troas to Caesarea. After touching at Sidon, the ship followed the coast of Syria until it was abreast of Cyprus, then it took an oblique course westward between Cyprus and the southern extremity of rockbound Cilicia. Leaving the wide bay of Attaleia on their right, the travellers rounded the point of the Chelidonian islands and reached Andriake (Pl. 7a) on the

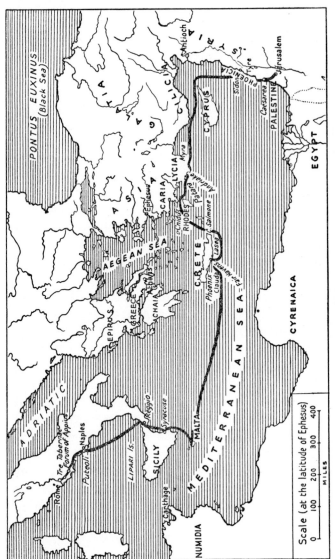

IV. ST. PAUL'S JOURNEY AS A PRISONER

Lycian coast. Andriake was the port of the important city of Myra, situated in the interior of the country which forms the estuary of the Myrus, and at the foot of cliffs full of rock-cut tombs. There were frequent sailings from Andriake, and the centurion Julius found an Alexandrian ship bound for Puteoli with a cargo of grain. He therefore left the ship of Andramyttium and put his prisoners on the Egyptian ship. The narrative of Acts does not tell us whether St. Paul availed himself of the opportunity to preach the gospel in a city which had hitherto lain beyond the scope of his itineraries. It is an attractive speculation, even if, in Byzantine Myra, the figure of St. Nicholas has wholly ousted that of the first apostle.

Meanwhile time was passing, and the violent storms which, in Lycia, bring the fine weather to an end, swelling the rivers and turning the low-lying plains into marshes, made sailing slow and difficult. Often, as I sailed along the wild and broken shores of this delightful country, have I pictured to myself the stages of St. Paul's last journey: the narrow entrance to Kekova, a closed harbour whose unruffled waters mirror the strange labyrinth of ogival tombs adorning the hillside, the roadstead of Antiphellos, crowned by the austere outlines of a Hellenistic theatre. Further west lies Patara with its imposing ruins buried in the sand; here is the estuary of the Xanthus, and far inland, on rising ground, are the twin acropolises of the ancient Lycian capital. Finally, here are the Seven Capes with their frowning cliffs, and so we pass into the deep bay of Telmessus, whose clear and peaceful waters afford a welcome rest to the traveller.

After sailing for several days between Rhodes and the Carian coast, the Alexandrian ship came abreast of Cnidus. It appears that the captain of the ship had intended to land at this port, but a north-east gale had driven him very far from the coast. They soon sighted Cape Salmone at the eastern end of Crete, and in order to gain shelter from the Aegean winds the ship skirted the southern coast of the island as far as Fair Havens near Lasea. St. Paul was of the opinion that the voyage should be discontinued at this point, but the captain decided to winter farther west at Phoenix which was thought to have a better harbour. We know that he was prevented from carrying out his plan by a frightful storm, and that the ship with the apostle on board barely succeeded in reaching Malta.

St. Paul and his companions remained three months at Malta, resuming their journey in February of the following year. Placed on board an Alexandrian ship, they first of all reached Syracuse, then Reggio in Calabria, and finally Puteoli, to the west of Naples. The rest of the journey was made by land. The rumour of the apostle's arrival had reached Rome, and the disciples came as far as Appii Forum and Tre Tabernae to meet him. About the middle of February in the year A.D. 60, St. Paul entered Rome as a prisoner.

The last stage of the journey and St. Paul's sojourn in the imperial capital lie outside my proposed limits. Moreover, from this point the evidence becomes extremely uncertain, and everything that has been written about St. Paul's missionary activities in the west seems to be mainly hypothetical. At this point, however, it may be of interest to attempt a summary of what had been accomplished since Paul and Barnabas took ship at Seleucia for Cyprus and Pamphylia. The apostolic message had reached an extremely varied audience. It had been heard by Lycaonian and Phrygian hillmen, burghers of Philippi, Jews of Beroea, merchants of Corinth or Ephesus. Although the last journey was made by a prisoner whose extraordinary personal magnetism won him fresh converts, yet the three previous missions had been carried out by a man who, though continually pursued, managed to retain his freedom. The contrast between the two stages of the apostle's missionary career is a touching one, and no less striking is the difference between the detailed narrative which we possess of the Greek period, and the abrupt silence which falls on the Roman period. Although the greatest caution must be exercised when dealing with the apostle's Roman period, the study of St. Paul's journeys through the Greek Orient will always be essential for anyone who wishes to become acquainted with the amazing progress of Christianity during its earliest period.

CHRONOLOGY OF ST. PAUL'S MISSIONARY JOURNEYS

Start of the first missionary journey	Spring of 44
Mission to Pamphylia, Pisidia and Lycaonia	44-47(?)
Stay at Antioch	47(?)-49
Start of the second missionary journey	Spring of 49
Macedonian mission	Winter 49-50
Corinthian mission	Spring of 50 to Autumn of 51
Return to Jerusalem	Autumn of 51
Start of the third missionary journey	Spring of 52
Sojourn in Galatia and in Phrygia	52-53
Ephesian mission	Spring of 53 to Spring of 56
Macedonian journey	Summer-Autumn 56
Second stay in Corinth	Winter 56-57
Journey from Corinth to Jerusalem by way of Macedonia and Troas	Spring of 57

Arrival at Jerusalem   Pentecost 57

Departure of St. Paul as a   September 59
   prisoner for Rome
Winter at Malta   Winter 59-60
Arrival at Rome   February 60

SELECT BIBLIOGRAPHY

Ramsay, Sir W. M.	*St. Paul the Traveller and Roman Citizen*, 1895.
——	*The Church in the Roman Empire*, 1904.
Harnack, A.	*The Mission and Expansion of Christianity*, Vol. I, 1908.
Lake, K. and Jackson, F.	*The Beginnings of Christianity*, Vol. IV, 1933.
Lake, K.	*The Earlier Epistles of St. Paul*, 1930.
Bevan, E.	*Hellenism and Christianity*, 1930.
Magie, D.	*The Roman Rule in Asia Minor*, 1950.
Cumont, F.	*Oriental Religions in Roman Paganism*, 1911.
Bruce, F. F.	*The Acts of the Apostles*, 1953.
——	*The Dawn of Christianity*, 1950.
Blunt, A. W. F.	*The Clarendon New Testament*, 'The Acts of the Apostles'.
Nock, A. D.	*St. Paul*, 1938.
Klausner, J.	*From Jesus to Paul*, 1942.